The Least of These

Wild Baby Bird Rescue Stories

Joan Harris

Foreword by Jane Goodall

WEST WINDS PRESS®

For my twin sister, June, who provides unfailing encouragement and a discerning eye. For Marty, my sister who lives just down the street. For my sons, Roe and Olen. And for my husband and best friend, Tom.

A portion of the proceeds from the sale of The Least of These will be donated to each of the wildlife rehabilitation centers discussed in this book.

ACKNOWLEDGMENTS—Special thanks go to John Parks, Hope Douglas, Pete Stevens, Peggy Coontz, Jan Goldman, Scott Smith, Bobby and Gloria Beckman, Jim Scott, Lynda White, Erin Estell, Mary Powell-McConnell, Shawnee Riplog-Peterson, Alan Lieberman, Cyndi Kuehler, Marla Kuhn, Meryl Faulkner, Tammy Conkle, Karen Jeffries, Libby Osnes-Erie, Jane Seitz, Tony Amos, Diann Bunnell, Gerry Gage, Janet and Lewis Miller, Fran Darnton, Ann Burke, and Sara Zimorski. Without their help, this book never would have happened. And my gratitude goes to Ellen Wheat for her skillful and sensitive editing. For her inspiration, and for her work on behalf of all those who cannot speak for themselves, I wish to express my deep gratitude to Jane Goodall. Information concerning the work carried on by the Jane Goodall Institute can be found at *www.janegoodall.org*.

Published by WestWinds Press®
An imprint of Graphic Arts Center Publishing Company
P.O. Box 10306, Portland, Oregon 97296-0306, 503-226-2402
www.gacpc.com

Library of Congress Cataloging-in-Publication Data
Harris, Joan, 1946-
  The least of these : wild baby bird rescue stories / by Joan Harris ; foreword by Jane Goodall.
    p. cm.
  ISBN 1-55868-860-9 (softbound)
  1. Birds—Conservation—United States. 2. Birds—Infancy—United States. 3. Wildlife rescue—United States.
I. Title.
  QL676.55.H37 2005
  639.9'78—dc22   2004012087

President/Publisher: Charles M. Hopkins
Associate Publisher: Douglas A. Pfeiffer
Editorial Staff: Timothy W. Frew, Tricia Brown, Kathy Howard, Jean Bond-Slaughter
Production Staff: Richard L. Owsiany, Susan Dupere
Cover Design: Elizabeth Watson
Interior Design: Jean Andrews
Copy Editor: Ellen Wheat

Printed in the United States of America

Contents

FOREWORD

The Least of These is a book that will immediately appeal to old and young alike, with its simple, engaging, and authoritative text, and its stunning illustrations. And because of the subjects themselves.

There is something utterly fascinating about birds—think how popular bird watching has become in so many countries around the world. My own love of birds began when I was a very small child—there are photos showing me crouched and intent as I fed pigeons and house sparrows at age two or three. And then, when I was four years old I was taken to spend a holiday on a farm. And, apparently, I began asking everyone where, on a hen, was the hole big enough for the egg to come out? Not getting a satisfactory reply I hid in a small, stuffy henhouse, covered with straw, for three or four hours—until finally a hen climbed in and laid her egg!

During the same visit I was asked to help care for a duck whose neck had been damaged by an angry goose. I nursed that duck, persuading her to eat, keeping her in my bedroom—and she got well. After that it seems I was always being asked to care for some little bird who had fallen from its nest, or an adult who had temporarily stunned itself by flying into a window. And I would search for nests and then go back day after day to crouch in a variety of uncomfortable positions in order to record when the babies hatched, and how frequently, and with what, the parent birds fed their young. I still remember vividly the moonlit night when I watched two young barn owls learning to fly—because the mother dived down and actually struck my head!

It is because of this kind of fascination with birds that, so often, when some tragedy befalls a nest, or a chick, there is someone who notices, and cares enough to want to help. (It is unfortunate that some baby birds are "rescued" needlessly—had they been left their mothers would likely have returned, but even that is better than simply not caring.)

Today there are a number of rescue and rehabilitation centers throughout North America—and indeed, in many countries around the world. Places where baby birds are taken in, nursed back to health and, whenever possible, released back into the wild. This captivating book describes the hard work, the patience, the love and the extraordinary expertise of the staff at some of these centers. Each story is enchanting, capturing not only the characteristics of the species, but the personalities of the different baby birds. But it is Joan Harris's illustrations that make this book so special. What a delight! Meticulously drawn, and capturing the essence of the different individuals. So lifelike you can almost imagine them sitting in front of you begging for attention, or replete, at peace and without a care in the world.

Indeed, the concept of the book—the stories and the illustrations—is brilliant. Our hearts are touched. There is sadness, joy, and humor. And wonderful descriptions of dedicated humans going to extraordinary lengths to care for the minutest scraps of flesh and budding feather. And the book is not only captivating, but educational also, giving up-to-date information about some of the responsible centers that help to care for our wild birds.

A real treasure that you will want on your coffee table and in your child's bookshelf.

—Jane Goodall

INTRODUCTION

The Caretakers

From early childhood, I have been fascinated by baby birds. Each year when springtime arrived at my grandparents' ranch, I watched and listened with wonder as an abundance of downy chicks also arrived. And I was intrigued to learn how much baby birds differ from their parents, both in appearance and voice.

In recent years, I decided to draw a series of the wild feathered youngsters I had met. And I had become interested in telling the stories of particularly memorable chicks that had either been rescued by rehabilitation centers or had been involved in species recovery efforts. In the spring of 2000, my mother sent me an article from her local newspaper about an abandoned turkey vulture chick being cared for at the Pueblo Raptor Center in Colorado. Accompanying the article was a remarkable photograph of the chick, named Hurlly. His fuzzy white wings were spread wide, his feet were planted sturdily underneath him, and his head was held low as he gazed defiantly at the camera. I had never seen a baby vulture, and was enthralled.

Most of us rarely have the opportunity to look closely at a baby bird—especially a wild baby bird—and the photograph offered a special visual insight. I couldn't put the little vulture's image out of my mind, and soon afterward I found myself at work on Hurlly's portrait and starting this book.

While doing research for the book, I came across so many people with a deep love and respect for birds. But even more than that, I found that people involved in wildlife rehabilitation translate that love into astounding gifts of time and energy. The satisfaction they receive when a bird is released into the wild, or when they save a life that would otherwise slip away, is their reward.

Stories from thirteen wildlife rehabilitation centers make up this book, from all parts of the United States including Hawaii and Alaska. The centers are large and small, and work with an amazing variety of birds. Fittingly, the smallest of the centers, Wildlife Rehabilitation of Northwest Tucson, successfully raises abandoned bumblebee-sized hummingbird chicks each spring. On the other end of the spectrum, the International Crane Foundation in Wisconsin is involved in bringing back five-foot-tall whooping cranes from the brink of extinction.

Several of these stories concern endangered species, and two of the baby birds included here are counted among the rarest creatures on earth. The Keauhou Bird Center is successfully breeding the critically endangered alala, a small inky-black crow that is native only to Hawaii. Likewise, the story of the whooping crane's recovery is one of the most heartwarming in the annals of endangered species. New York's Cornell Raptor Center is engaged in a program to breed the increasingly rare accipiters (forest-dwelling hawks). Even the military is involved with helping endangered birds. When tiny California least terns began nesting on the beaches of Coronado Island, setting up nurseries in areas needed for amphibious training, the Navy responded by establishing a unique partnership with Project Wildlife.

Humor is liberally sprinkled throughout daily happenings in wildlife rehabilitation settings. I have found it even in centers engaged in scholarly scientific efforts to propagate rare species of birds. Alan Lieberman, a biologist with the Keauhou Bird Center, related an incident involving a pair of alala. While visiting their aviary in Maui, Alan slipped quietly into an observation room hoping to watch the pair's natural behavior. Knowing that the intelligent crows were always well aware of visitors, he stayed still and quiet inside the small sheet-metal room trying to fool the birds into thinking no one was there. The day was hot, and by the end of an hour Alan was quite uncomfortable. Deciding enough time had passed, he peeked through a crack in the sheet metal to look for the alala, but they weren't in sight. Glancing up, he saw two attentive pairs of eyes. The alala had been watching him through a screw hole in the top of the observation room.

Unexpected happenings are the norm in these centers, as well. Wildlife Rehabilitation of Northwest Tucson released a great horned owl named Stanley in the spring of 2000, after rearing him from downy chickhood. With his distinctive hoots and outgoing nature, he had endeared himself to the entire staff. Two years after Stanley's release, a wild owl took up residence in a tall pine tree behind the center. Looking down expectantly with enormous gold eyes, he set up a racket each evening as if expecting a dinner of mice to be served. The amused staff identified Stanley by his unmistakable *hoo-hoo*s. Accompanied by a wild mate, he set about building a nest. The chosen spot was inside a large dog kennel used by the staff to transport injured birds to and from the veterinarian. This proved an inconvenience when Stanley (who turned out to be female and was renamed Estancia) raised her three owl chicks in the backyard and protected the territory from human intruders. And she continued to beg the staff for mice each evening, using the offerings to feed her brood.

Because specific licensing is required to legally care for wildlife, if you find an injured or abandoned baby bird, it is important to locate a rehabilitation facility. Most communities have such clinics, which often start with a single kindhearted veterinarian volunteering his or her time to treat injured birds and animals. Following the *Exxon Valdez* oil spill, Dr. Jim Scott established the Bird Treatment and Learning Center (Bird TLC) in Anchorage in the back room of his animal hospital. Today, this center is housed in a large warehouse and staffed by a cadre of dedicated volunteers. And Anchorage residents know exactly where to take an injured wild bird.

Many baby birds that do not need help are "rescued" by well-meaning people. Often, the fledgling's parents are close by, collecting food for their young. Should you find a baby bird on the ground, remove cats or dogs from the area, and quietly observe from a distance to see whether the parents return. If they don't come back within four to six hours, you can assume the baby is abandoned. Contact a licensed wildlife rehabilitator for advice, and in the meantime do not attempt to feed water, which can enter the lungs and cause pneumonia. Baby songbirds, in most cases, need only be placed gently back in their nests, while raptor babies will need immediate specialized care from a rehabilitation center. There is no need to worry about leaving your scent on the baby birds, because birds generally have a poor sense of smell, and the parents will not reject their offspring because it was handled by humans. Hummingbird mothers do not sit on their nests, but fly in to feed the babies four to six times each hour; watch the nest continuously for one hour before assuming the babies are abandoned. And the babies of ground-nesting birds, such as terns, plovers, and vultures, may actually be on the nest, if you find them on the beach or forest floor.

Should you wish to volunteer time at a wildlife rehabilitation center in your own community, you will find your efforts are genuinely appreciated. Though not everyone can volunteer time, almost without exception these centers need funding to help with the feeding and care of feathered residents. Whether you "adopt" a whooping crane with a donation to the International Crane Foundation, contribute funds to help build Cornell University's new hawk barn, or provide a month's worth of mice for a vulture at the Pueblo Raptor Center, you will find that your funds are well used and appreciated. It is possible to give in the form of birthday or holiday gifts of memberships, adoption certificates, or donations to the center of your choice.

This book is a small tribute to all of the staff and volunteers who give their passion and their talents to wildlife rescue.

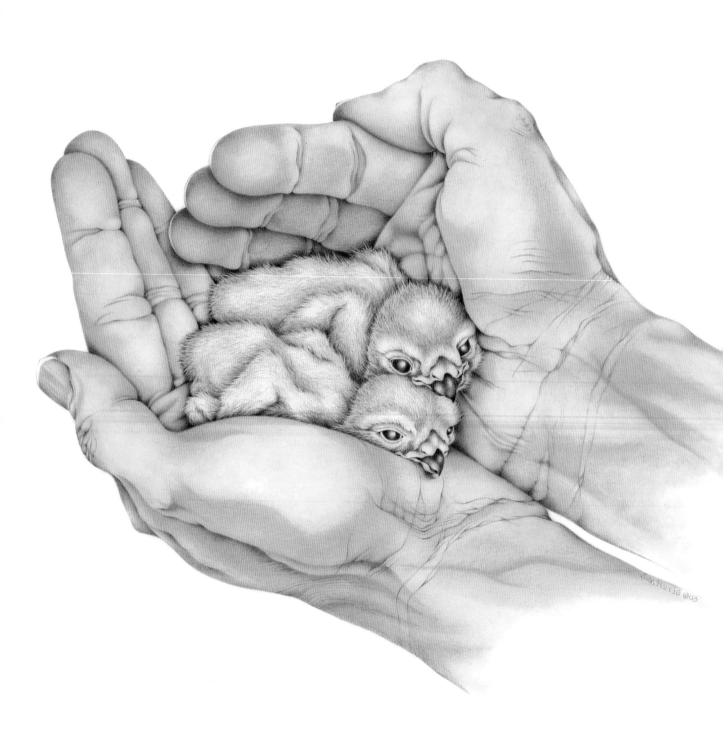

Founder

SHARP-SHINNED HAWK

Cornell Raptor Program, Ithaca, New York

Stepping softly across a carpet of moss, John Parks headed for a dense stand of red pines. He had been alerted to the presence of a sharp-shinned hawk in the area by the high-pitched *kik-kik-kik-kik* of the resident female. While not as aggressive as their larger cousin, the northern goshawk—known to literally strike human intruders—both male and female sharpies defiantly guard a fifty-yard radius around their nest tree. Quick and agile, they appear and disappear among the pines.

Identifying the nest tree, even within a small territory, is a challenge, but John was well acquainted with sharpies. A professor of animal science at Cornell University and the director of the Cornell Raptor Program, he had extensive knowledge of these relatively small, feisty hawks. Just ahead he spotted their plucking post, a stump where the reclusive woodland hawks bring their quarry to pluck

and dismember it. Beneath this post, strewn on the dark forest floor, was evidence of how successful these little hunters are—tufts of bright yellow and blue feathers, colorful remains of warblers caught and dispatched. Quietly, John looked at the bases of nearby pines for evidence of droppings. Finding some, he peered up through the dense, interlocking branches for a nest.

Raptor biologists always excel at tree climbing. Only after ascending several feet up the tree could he see the small platform of sticks in the upper branches. While climbing, John kept a wary eye out for the winged van-guard. As he pulled himself level with the nest, a beautiful blue-gray adult exited almost silently over the side. Her retreat revealed a solitary, white downy chick who returned the stranger's gaze with large, black eyes. Less than a day old, the hatchling snuggled beside two pale, brown mottled eggs. Reaching gently into the nest, John scooped up the small chick, cupping the almost weightless bit of fluff in his hand as he climbed back down the tree. He had been granted permission from state wildlife authorities to acquire several young sharp-shinned hawks from the wild, but this hatchling was the first and only sharpie taken from the nest for inclusion in Cornell's program.

It was the spring of 1993, and the Cornell Raptor Program was itself still a fledgling. Created to allow a unique hands-on opportunity for students in conservation and veterinary or animal science, the program was housed in the legendary Hawk Barn. Once home to the famous Peregrine Fund breeding project that successfully brought back peregrine falcons from the brink of extinction in the 1970s, the facility now hosted the three species of accipiters—goshawks, Cooper's hawks, and sharp-shinned hawks—in wood-paneled, spacious enclosures within this captive breeding facility. The fact that accipiters are not officially endangered, though goshawks are uncommon, made it possible to involve students in these raptors' everyday care. And because these hawks are indigenous to central New York, young birds raised in the program could be freed locally. The tiny chick cupped protectively in John's hands, weighing in at a mere half-ounce, was destined to become

the crucial cornerstone of this exceptional program. Though birds are seldom named at Cornell, this special little fellow would always be known as the founder male.

Arriving home with the downy hatchling, John was aware of the round-the-clock care this tiny creature would need. Nestling the baby carefully into a rubber tub lined with a soft towel, he adjusted an incandescent lamp above the chick and turned his attention to chef duties. Taking a defrosted quail out of the refrigerator, he plucked, skinned, and minced the meat along with soft organs and small bones, and added a liberal sprinkling of calcium powder. Then, using long forceps, John picked up a small drop of the concoction and turned to the makeshift nest. Newly hatched sharpie chicks can swallow only minute bits of food; their mouths are barely the size of a child's fingernail. With bobbing head reminiscent of a dashboard ornament, the small creature hungrily opened his beak wide for the tidbit of quail. Smiling down at the tiny chick, John knew these minced offerings would be needed five times daily.

Sharpie chicks grow rapidly. Within a month, John settled the newcomer into a hawk barn aviary stocked generously with toys and sticks. Involved now in a process called "dual imprinting," the youngster was exposed to other sharpies while still being fed by John. These high-strung birds adapt better if they imprint on humans; but the fledgling could also retain a good degree of his inborn wildness by associating with feathered cohorts. Several females, rehabilitated but unable to fly, already resided in aviaries. The young male's arrival in their midst did not go unnoticed.

By the next spring, his eye coloration began changing to the adult's blood red, and his breast already bore the rufous streaks worn by a mature male. His sleek plumage bore promise of a handsome dark blue-gray coloration. For the first time, sharpie courtship activities were well under way in the hawk barn.

At the end of each season, using an age-old falconry technique called hacking, students under John's tutelage provide artificial nests and food until the young sharpies are self-sufficient and able to fly free. For Cornell students, releases are always bittersweet. But the hawks impart valuable lessons. And to this day, these feathered teachers descend from a single unbroken bloodline, passed on by the founder male.

SHARP-SHINNED HAWK (Accipiter striatus):
  Nest: Constructed yearly of sturdy twigs, lined with bark chips.
      Usually in thick groves of conifers, 10–60 ft. up in a tree.
  Eggs: Bluish white, elliptical, splotched with brown,
      1.5 x 1.18 in.
  Clutch size: Normally 4–5 eggs, rarely 3–8.
      Single brooded.
  Incubation: Both parents; hatch in 30–35 days.
  Nestling: Semialtricial chicks, covered in creamy
      white down. Weight 0.53–0.63 oz. at hatch;
      by 5–6 weeks, males approximately 3.15 oz.,
      females approximately 5.6 oz.
  Food: Mostly songbirds, plucked free of feathers.
  Nestling period: Tended by female, who receives food from male.
      Young fly in 23 days, dependent on parents for 1 more month.
  Adult: 9–13 in. long, 17–23-in. wingspan, weight 3.07–7.7 oz. Bluish
      upperparts, rufous or tawny buff underparts, with barring.

HEAD OF ADULT SHARP-SHINNED HAWK

Faith

MUTE SWAN

Wind Over Wings, Clinton, Connecticut

Snapping turtles and mute swans share the waters of Candlewood Lake, and their encounters can be disastrous. One spring afternoon, a downy gray cygnet had fallen behind her siblings, and was paddling furiously to catch up. Ahead, two elegant swans slipped along the water's edge looking for tender shoots and buds. Their babies, cloaked in waterproof down, dived and bobbed back up to the surface. Some cygnets floated lazily, resting a webbed foot atop their back. Waiting by the lake's edge with an offering of breadcrumbs, an enraptured little girl giggled at the young swans' antics. But the child wasn't the only one interested in the cygnets.

A mature snapping turtle is a formidable predator. Cruising underwater, and attracted to a potential meal by the enticing splash of webbed feet, the turtle likely recognized an opportunity. The startled child saw the turtle's attack, which cut off the little swan's beak and cracked her skull. But the injured baby was about to begin an odyssey that would deeply touch all who met her.

Horrified at what she had seen, the youngster ran up to her shorefront home. Hearing the breathless child's story, her mother knew the cygnet's survival depended on getting help quickly. One local resident, Mary Louden, was well known for her volunteer work with injured wildlife. During regular springtime visits to the lake, she always offered treats of Pepperidge Farm Goldfish crackers to the mute swan family. Arriving at the shore with her pockets full of the orange morsels, Mary tossed out a handful of crackers and watched anxiously as the swans glided near, followed by the injured youngster. The downy baby, hungry but unable to feed, lingered under some low branches after her family had eaten their fill. Literally climbing out on a limb, Mary deftly reached down and scooped up the cygnet.

At the veterinary office, Dr. John Robb opened the cardboard box, gently lifted out the small swan, and cradled her in his lap. Badly disfigured, the cygnet had little chance of survival; yet she met the doctor's gaze steadily with wide, intelligent eyes. *This baby,* thought the vet, *hasn't given up on living.* And he wouldn't give up on her either.

At Wind Over Wings, a wildlife rehabilitation center in the nearby town of Clinton, director Hope Douglas was on the phone. Her heart sank as she listened, knowing that it would take a miracle for this cygnet to survive. Yet Dr. Robb was describing how well the delicate surgery had gone, and even more amazingly, was discussing the matter of a new beak. This little swan, he explained, had faith that she was going to make it. Driving to pick up the cygnet, Hope mulled over Dr. Robb's comment. Perhaps, she thought, she might call the small survivor Faith.

Back at the rehab center, Hope readied a mixture of greens and soft corn in the blender. Waiting patiently at her feet, the cygnet peered curiously at the proceedings. With her wide-set black eyes, velvet gray down, and blue-tinged webbed feet, Faith was not at all the "ugly duckling" of fairy tales. Holding a bright red feeding tube attached to a large syringe full of liquid food, Hope sat down on the floor beside the hungry cygnet. Tube feeding can be stressful for all involved, but Faith stood calmly as Hope's skillful hands carefully threaded in the slender red tube.

Taking hourly feedings in stride, the swan soon unveiled a surprising new skill. As Hope bent down to offer a freshly blended breakfast, Faith eagerly took over by swallowing the tube on her own. Equating food with this now familiar experience, the youngster grew rapidly.

Prosthetic beaks are not a common item, and fashioning one both lightweight and sturdy enough for a full-grown mute swan would not be easy. When Hope asked Dr. Tom Brady for help, Faith trustingly allowed an examination. Starting with molded impressions, and working in collaboration with other specialists, Tom meticulously created a hinged beak out of the same acrylic used in orthodontic retainers for humans.

When injured cygnets arrive each spring at Wind Over Wings now, they find a tender foster mother in Faith. Able to eat normally again, she demonstrates feeding techniques to her adoptive broods, partaking along with them from fresh servings of smelt and bluefish. The youngsters watch with excitement as she playfully rattles prized goldfish crackers in her acrylic beak before gulping them down. Mute swans are by no means mute, though their voices are seldom heard. The comparative silence of these swans has resulted in this misnomer. Calling to her charges with quiet notes only audible nearby, Faith uses her unique vocabulary to gather the cygnets protectively under her wings with urgent calls, or beckon them to dinner with soft noises.

A spirited survivor in spite of overwhelming odds, and helped along the way by many caring hands, Faith has become a teacher in other ways as well. Now familiar with educational trips to classrooms, she obviously relishes the encounters. While Hope provides species information, children can experience firsthand the considerable presence of an enormous and graceful swan. Having developed her own routine, Faith usually begins by spreading her great wings and fanning the room. Then, she slowly begins to walk up and down the aisles, as though coyly inviting close-up inspection of her marvelous new beak.

MUTE SWAN (Cygnus olor):
>   Nest: 4–5 feet wide, heaped with plant material, hollow in center. Constructed at water's edge or on a reedbed in shallows.
>   Eggs: Vary from pure white to pale blue-gray or green tinted, 4.45 x 2.91 in.
>   Clutch size: Normally 3–5 eggs, as many as 7. Single brooded.
>   Incubation: 34–38 days, primarily by female.
>   Nestling: Precocial cygnets covered with dense white or grayish down. Weight 7.63 oz. at hatch (25% is yolk sac).
>   Food: Aquatic vegetation and grain, small amphibians, aquatic invertebrates.
>   Nestling period: Cygnets leave nest in 2 days, following adults on water. Fiercely protected by parents, independent at 4 mo.
>   Adult: 50–60 in. long, 82–94-in. wingspan, weight 22 lb. All white.

HEAD OF ADULT MUTE SWAN

Hurlly

TURKEY VULTURE

Pueblo Raptor Center, Pueblo, Colorado

It was a child who discovered the small vulture chick. He was standing his ground, feet planted defiantly apart, head lowered, and oversized wings outstretched. The abandoned baby, in spite of his warning hisses, was defenseless and in trouble. Crouching low, the little boy squealed with delight as the tiny creature eyed him curiously then sidled up to tug on his shoelaces. As though picking up a fragile toy, the child gathered up the baby bird and headed breathlessly for home.

Healthy turkey vulture chicks are always spotlessly clean and completely odorless, with a dense coat of white down. This chick was not only filthy, but was also covered with lice and fleas. As Nancy Kelly ushered the little boy and his mother into Second Chance Wildlife Rehabilitation that evening, she gazed with dismay at the squirming dingy bundle cradled in the child's arms. Nancy recognized that this baby was an orphan, and he was the smallest turkey vulture she had ever seen.

Filling the sink with a few inches of warm water and gentle soap, Nancy lowered the protesting baby into the suds. While deftly rubbing his tiny body, she explored for wounds, and was relieved to find none. Even without injuries, an abandoned chick rarely survives long in the wild before being taken by a predator or succumbing to cold and starvation. Toweling off the bedraggled creature, Nancy suddenly felt something drip down under her blouse, and she couldn't help but chuckle. Indignant and wet, the little bird had used the traditional defense mechanism of vultures—regurgitation—and his aim was quite good. Perhaps, thought Nancy, this baby could be named for his talent; she would call him Hurlly.

Knowing the small creature would need specialized care, Nancy telephoned the Pueblo Raptor Center the next morning. Housed in a converted pig barn built solidly out of local limestone in the 1930s, the center had cared for vultures before. These gracefully soaring creatures had become more populous in recent years in southern Colorado's skies, and occasionally were brought to the clinic needing medical care. Predominantly scavengers, vultures play an important environmental role as the planet's garbage disposals. Always a favorite among the center's volunteers, these birds are gentle and nonaggressive, rarely quarreling even when feeding in groups. Settling arguments without violence is to their benefit, as damage to their huge wings might limit their ability to glide effortlessly while searching for food.

Already able to eat on his own, the youngster eagerly accepted defrosted and minced mice from Peggy Coontz, a raptor biologist at the center. Before long he was fiercely defending both food and nest box with a warning series of muted wheezes and snorts that comprise a vulture's vocabulary. But young birds in foster care quickly imprint on the humans who nurture them; soon Hurlly would no longer identify with others of his own kind. Peggy realized that a proper role model was necessary.

A call to the Pueblo Zoo resulted in the loan of a male turkey vulture, named Morgan, who became the chick's surrogate parent. A mature bird, Morgan sported red, bare skin on his deeply wrinkled neck and head. Nature's gift of baldness for vultures not only helps with hygiene, but also serves efficiently as a cooling system. With intelligent amber eyes, an ivory bill, and iridescent black feathers, Hurlly's foster dad was a handsome beast indeed.

As the summer months passed, hopes were raised that Hurlly could be successfully released. With Morgan as a roommate, daily tutelage in vulture culture had progressed well. Hurlly had exchanged his spectacular white baby fuzz for dark glossy feathers, and his massive wings would easily negotiate the classic glides needed to search for carrion. Plans were made to release him close to a wild flock living in a nearby river bottom.

The day they set Hurlly free, Peggy felt the familiar lump in her throat as she watched him circling lazily in the blue Colorado sky. She hoped he had learned his lessons well. But it wasn't long before some strange reports started trickling in about a large black bird acting in an unusual way.

Scott Smith, a reporter for the *Pueblo Chieftain*, was enjoying the Bluegrass festival at the Nature Center when something startling caught his eye. Unruffled by hundreds of human music-lovers, and displaying very unvulture-like behavior, Hurlly was frolicking with kids on the riverbank and boldly begging for funnel cakes. What struck Scott was the vulture's obvious attraction to children. Whether beak-to-nose with them on the jungle gym, or splashing across the shallow creek in a spirited game of follow-the-leader, the young bird seemed irresistibly drawn to youngsters. Scott made a mental note to talk to the Raptor Center on Monday.

In the weeks that followed, Vulture 101 became front-page news. But as time slipped by, and Hurlly continued to prefer children's company to that of his own kind, freedom no longer remained a safe option for him. His trust and lack of wildness could expose him to risk. Today, Hurlly still interacts with children often, going about his business as an education bird. Visiting classrooms, he brightens noticeably when he spies the small humans he adores. Fitted with a special harness, he struts excitedly among giggling grade-schoolers, reveling in their attention. And, just perhaps, he is helping an entire community change its mind about the species known as vultures.

TURKEY VULTURE (Cathartes aura):
>   Nest: Eggs laid on bare ground in secluded spot.
>   Eggs: Creamy white, marked liberally with brown splotches, 2.8 x 1.93 in.
>   Clutch size: Usually 2 eggs, sometimes 1, rarely 3. Single brooded.
>   Incubation: Both parents, 37–41 days.
>   Nestling: Semialtricial, covered with long white
>   down. Head mostly bare, showing black skin
>   underneath. Weight 2.1 oz. at hatch.
>   Food: Both adults regurgitate carrion
>   for chicks.
>   Nestling period: Youngsters grow feathers
>   slowly, fly at approximately 11 weeks.
>   Adult: 26 in. long, 67-in. wingspan,
>   weight 4 lb. Head and neck bare, pinkish
>   or red. Plumage brownish black with slight iridescence.

HEAD OF ADULT TURKEY VULTURE

Squirt

SANDHILL CRANE

Bird Treatment and Learning Center (Bird TLC), Anchorage, Alaska

From the bottom of the knit hat that cradled him snugly, the tiny sandhill crane peered up curiously at Bobby Beckman. Only hours old, the chick was the single survivor from a clutch of two eggs. It was late Friday afternoon at the Bird Treatment and Learning Center (TLC) and Bobby had just opened the door to a soldier, who gently handed over his knitted camouflage hat with its unusual cargo.

During training that day on the range at Fort Richardson, Alaska, artillery fire had landed close to the undiscovered ground nest. Nearly five feet in diameter, it consisted simply of a large heap of plant material thrown in from around the site, lined thinly with grass. When soldiers found the scattered pieces of the nest, only one egg remained undamaged. The lieutenant carefully scooped up the egg, storing it in his hat for protection and slipping it under his shirt for warmth. At home several hours later, he gently laid the hat, with its fragile contents, on his kitchen table. Then something quite unexpected happened; the egg hatched.

A sandhill crane chick resembles an orange ball of fluff atop already spindly legs. An "egg tooth" perches on the dark tip of its smooth, pinkish bill; used like a pick to help the chick break free from its shell, the egg tooth will fall off within a few days. Small enough to be held in the palm of a hand, the baby would rapidly grow to be an imposing crane over four feet tall. Looking him over closely, Bobby knew he was accepting a round-the-clock undertaking. Unable to hold up his head properly or stand on his own, this chick needed immediate nourishment and warmth to survive.

A college student at the University of Alaska, Bobby had already been a volunteer at

Bird TLC for several years. He was no novice at caring for injured birds. His love for wild creatures had been encouraged by his mother, Gloria, who would also play a part in the young crane's care. Bundling up the tiny wisp of orange fuzz, Bobby closed the clinic up for the night and headed home with the chick tucked into a laundry basket. Such a tiny squirt, thought Bobby, as he smiled down at his charge; it was a name that stuck.

The Bird TLC clinic had never before admitted a sandhill crane, making this newly hatched member of the most ancient of all bird species an uncommon sight. Though the least endangered of all crane species, sandhills still number only 500,000 worldwide. Crane parents fiercely guard their shallow grass-lined ground nests, protecting their speckled olive-buff eggs and chicks from predators and caring for them meticulously, so rehabilitation centers seldom take in their young. Flying thousands of miles north to raise their young in Alaska, sandhills are notably unfussy about their choice of nesting locations, often choosing dry areas rather than the swamps preferred by most cranes. The choice of this site, on a military training range, had been particularly unfortunate.

Gloria gasped when she first glimpsed her son's tiny houseguest; she knew they would need expert help to save the little bird. It was already late in the evening in Baraboo, Wisconsin, the headquarters of the International Crane Foundation. But her desperate call raised a volunteer, who doubted that Gloria held a rare sandhill crane in her hands. Crane chicks are vocal from the start, and this one was already making low purring calls interspersed with high-pitched peeps. Gloria held Squirt up to the phone. The surprised volunteer needed no further convincing.

Armed now both with recipes for appropriate food and explicit instructions for care, Bobby settled the little crane into a child's plastic swimming pool placed centrally in the family room. Soon Squirt was eating enthusiastically from a smorgasbord of mealworms and baby-bird food mix supplied by Bird TLC. Before long, goldfish and hard-boiled eggs appeared on the menu too, followed by defrosted whole mice and moistened dog food. With soft, fluttering chirps, the little crane begged for food. His primary adult voice would become the distinctive broken rattle that has echoed across the earth for millions of years. But for now the baby's cries resembled a chorus of frogs in a swamp.

Gaining nearly 3.5 ounces a day with good nutrition and care, Squirt began interacting and playing in earnest. Though very young, he displayed the ancient and complex form of behavior practiced by all cranes—he danced. An adult sandhill is capable of leaping twelve feet into the air during these ritualistic dances, which are used to establish pair bonds. With enthusiastic bows and leaps, Squirt invited his human companion to join in. To provide additional exercise, Bobby walked around the block of the housing area with the crane in tow. Before long, Bobby's tiny charge had stretched to an imposing three feet in height.

By summer's end, it was time to move Squirt to a permanent home. Imprinted as he was on humans and having lacked a crane role model, he could not safely be released into the wild. But Wild Life Images, a rehabilitation facility in Oregon located along the crane's migration flyway, had room to house him with another sandhill. With luck, he might yet become wild enough to fly free. And the next spring, when migrating flocks of sandhills would bugle noisily overhead, Bobby hoped that Squirt would be among them, 5,000 feet high and climbing.

SANDHILL CRANE (Grus canadensis):

Nest: 3–5 feet diameter, of plant material, hollowed in the middle, lined with grass.

Eggs: Pale buff or olive-buff, splotched with brown or lilac, 3.7 x 2.36 in.

Clutch size: Usually 2 eggs, but occasionally 1, rarely 3. Single brooded.

Incubation: Both parents, 30–32 days.

Nestling: Precocial, covered with buff down, underside whitish. Weight 4.31 oz. at hatch.

Food: Insects, snails, crustaceans, fish, amphibians, rodents, snails, plants.

Nestling period: Leave the nest soon after hatching, protected by both parents. Fly in 70 days, remain with adults for 1 year.

HEAD OF ADULT SANDHILL CRANE

Adult: (lesser) 41 in. long, 73-in. wingspan, weight 7.3 lb. Gray body, only crane with fully feathered neck and head except for bare red forecrown.

Hope / Liberty

BALD EAGLE

Audubon Center for Birds of Prey, Maitland, Florida

Huddled against the trunk of a slash pine tree, a bedraggled eaglet gazed steadily back at the woman crouching in front of her. Blown from her nest during a severe April thunderstorm, the youngster was unable to survive yet on her own. Though she had broken her fifty-foot tumble to the ground by spreading already huge wings, she was still too young to fly.

Lynda White, now down on one knee as she spoke soothingly to the eaglet, was no novice when it came to raptors. She was the EagleWatch coordinator for Florida's Audubon Center for Birds of Prey, an hour away in Maitland. Lynda knew this fledgling couldn't survive without help, but catching her might be difficult. Though only ten weeks old, the bird was fully feathered and nearly the size of an adult bald eagle. Slowly reaching for the young bird with protectively gloved hands,

Lynda sighed with relief as the eaglet allowed herself to be gathered up.

While her husband drove to Maitland, Lynda cradled the fledgling on her lap and kept a cautious grip on the bird's legs to immobilize the impressive set of talons. All bald eagles have the potential for dangerous ferocity, but this one seemed calm and relaxed, and as the miles slipped by without incident, Lynda was relieved.

A celebrity already, the eaglet had been watched continually by a videocam secured atop her enormous nest. Perched high in a huge pine, this nest in Saint Cloud, Florida, was the focus of the Audubon EagleWatch 2000 project, and had offered an intimate glimpse into bald eagle family life that spring. The massive structure of sticks and branches, twelve feet high and over eight feet across, was reused annually by the same mated pair of eagles. Lined generously with grass, plant stems, and pine needles, the nest provided a safe haven this year for two offspring. Thanks to cameras and funding provided by the *Orlando Sentinel,* fascinated onlookers followed the progress of the downy gray hatchlings. Red Huber, a photojournalist for the newspaper, treated readers to beautifully photographed articles on the growing chicks, laced with eagle lore and educational tidbits.

When both youngsters developed avian pox, a viral infection transmitted by mosquitoes, viewers immediately voiced concern. The Audubon Center explained that this was a naturally occurring ailment that can heal by itself, but monitored the situation closely. When one of the fledglings disappeared from view after the thunderstorm, Lynda immediately left to check on it.

The clinic lights showed how severe the eaglet's pox infection was. Gentle removal of scabs in her nostrils provided immediate relief for her labored breathing, but she would require laser surgery to speed healing. As Lynda and Heather, the center's veterinary technician, gently explored chocolate-brown feathers for signs of injury, they marveled at the youngster's calm nature. Regarding her caretakers with wide amber eyes, the young bird accepted ministrations of antibiotics and fluids without complaint. Otherwise well nourished and healthy, this juvenile bald eagle stood a good

chance of recovery and living in the wild again. Perhaps, Lynda thought, Hope would be an appropriate nickname.

Following surgery, housed comfortably in an indoor enclosure called a mews, Hope began a slow, steady recuperation. A small pond invited bathing, and squeaky rubberized toys provided enticing playthings. Soon the clinic staff discovered that the young eagle had definite dining preferences. Mackerel and rats were relished favorites, while chicken was always declined. By fall, Hope had grown more wary and eaglelike, cackling her annoyance when approached—a crucial survival skill. When the time came to move her to a large flight barn so she could practice aerial and raptor social skills, everyone knew her release was imminent.

A crisp morning in October found a group of Audubon Center staff, volunteers, and well-wishers gathered to bid farewell to Hope. Healthy once again thanks to many caring hands, and wearing a numbered aluminum identification band, she confidently took wing as Lynda tossed her into the air. Circling briefly before being joined by another eagle, Hope's maiden flight left most of the crowd teary-eyed.

Nearly two years would pass before the Audubon Center would have news of her again. When a rehab center in west Florida called about an injured bald eagle under their care, Lynda was stunned when they read the number off the bird's leg band. Sideswiped by a truck while eating a rabbit along the roadside, Hope's wing was badly damaged. Though she had lived successfully in the wild for two years, freedom no longer remained an option.

Wanting an excellent permanent home for Hope, the center contacted the National Aviary in Pittsburgh. The Animal Encounters program in the aviary allows visitors to interact with feathered residents. Handled now by Erin Estell, an aviculturist with a great love of raptors, the young eagle's mellow nature is serving her well in educational presentations. And behind the scenes, the aviary's staff has noted that Hope's culinary preferences have remained with her—she disdains offerings of chicken but will eagerly accept tidbits of mackerel. Not yet mature, she still wears the mottled brown and white feathers of a juvenile. Not until she is five years old will she dress in the pure white head feathers that make bald eagles so recognizable. Newly named Liberty, she is an ambassador of bald eagles, allowing students and audiences a rare close-up encounter with our national bird.

BALD EAGLE (Haliaeetus leucocephalus):

Nest: Up to 12 feet high x 8.5 feet across, at the top of a tall conifer or cliff, reused yearly, lined with pine needles, grass, leaves.

Eggs: Subelliptical, white, with slight gloss, 3.07 x 2.28 in.

Clutch size: Usually 2, occasionally 1–4. Single brooded.

Incubation: Both parents, occasionally just the female, 33–35 days.

Nestling: Semialtricial, covered by gray or cream-colored, long, thin down. Weight 3.96 oz. at hatch. Fastest growing bird in North America, can gain up to 5.95 oz./day.

Food: Fish or small mammals. Fed by male for the first 2 weeks.

Nestling period: Active by 10 days, move from nest at 56 days. Fly by 2.5 months, but rely on parents for 6 more weeks.

Adult: 30 in. long, 80-in. wingspan, weight 9.5–12 lb. (females larger). After about 5 years, dark brown plumage with white head and tail.

HEAD OF ADULT BALD EAGLE

Herman

BROWN PELICAN

Arizona-Sonora Desert Museum, Tucson, Arizona

Spotting a pelican in the heart of the Sonoran Desert seems like a mirage. Yet the juvenile brown pelican swimming in a sewer treatment pond in Nogales was a real bird. Concerned employees watched the youngster paddle in circles, on waters that held no promise of a fish dinner. Knowing the fledgling needed help, two workmen gathered up an old blanket and paddled out in a small boat to get the bird. But pelicans are agile on water, even when dehydrated and weak. It was several long hours before one of the men succeeded in lifting the exhausted creature safely out of the pond.

When Mary Powell-McConnell picked up the phone that afternoon, she smiled knowingly. As soon as the voice on the other end said "This is really going to sound crazy," she knew this was a wayward pelican call. A member of the quarantine staff at the Arizona-Sonora Desert Museum, Mary had played host to these birds before. During spring monsoons, juvenile pelicans sometimes make the trip from Mexican shores into Southern Arizona. Still inexperienced at both flying and navigating, they end up in the desert, usually so exhausted that they are unable to take off again. This young pelican, however, was lucky. Freshly rescued from the treatment pond, wrapped securely in a blanket, and nestled in a caring workman's lap, he was a front-seat passenger in a truck headed toward the museum an hour's drive north.

Pelicans are among the largest and heaviest flying birds. Because human desert dwellers are more accustomed to seeing tiny hummingbirds sipping at feeders, startled Tucson residents call the museum wondering what is in the pool in their front yard eating the koi. One spring, a white pelican turned up in the parking lot of a Roadway Inn. Another errant brown pelican honed in on Breakers Water Park, no doubt lured by the artificial waves. One bird was even spotted waddling alongside the I-10 freeway. When the young pelican from Nogales arrived at the museum that afternoon, Mary eagerly gathered him up. Pelicans were one of her favorite visitors, and with luck she would be able to give this one his freedom back.

Entering a large, private enclosure, Mary lowered the youngster to the floor and sat beside him to check him out. Often, following crash landings in the desert, pelicans arrive covered with cactus spines. Fortunately, this bird had escaped that painful experience. Newly fledged and barely beyond the baby stage, he peered at her curiously with large hazel eyes. California brown pelicans, though the smallest of pelican species, are imposing birds that can weigh up to ten pounds. With enormous seven-foot wingspans, these magnificent and graceful flyers soar at dizzying altitudes. Mary ran her skilled hands gently over her new charge, and discovered a soft tissue injury to his right wing that would require treatment. She also realized delousing was definitely in order for them both; the annoying parasites had already started hopping on her clothes and hair. Standing up, she couldn't help but smile at the newcomer. Crouching low and fluttering, he eyed her expectantly while noisily uttering a baby pelican's begging call.

Housed comfortably in a spacious concrete pen equipped with a large tank of clean water, the young bird soon discovered that there was no shortage of smelt at the museum. Though most visiting pelicans are fussy eaters, requiring endless tempting or even force-feeding, this one opened his gaping beak obligingly. The liquid fish diet and fluids—usually Gatorade, which worked well and seemed palatable to even the most particular birds—was not necessary this time. Nicknamed Herman, the easygoing creature was soon indulged by the entire aviculture staff. Mary could even slip a vitamin D pill into his first smelt of the day. Before long, Herman was scooping fish out of the tank effortlessly, consuming three pounds a day of the silvery food.

Settling into his new routine, Herman's endearing ways captivated his caretakers. Nesting contentedly by day on a curled-up water hose, he raucously welcomed mealtimes with an animated series of dips and hops. Though restored to good health, Herman's wing injury needed time to heal. Eagerly anticipating twice-daily physical therapy sessions as a game, he patiently allowed Mary to exercise and strengthen his flight muscles. Carefully extending his wing out and away from his body, she moved it up and down in a flapping motion while Herman flapped his other wing in perfect rhythm. Birds requiring such intensive treatments often imprint on people, becoming too tame to successfully release. But pelicans have always had a close relationship with humans, and imprinting is less damaging in this species. Finally, nine months after his desert experience began, Mary was satisfied that Herman was ready for freedom.

Mary felt the familiar lump in her throat as she watched Herman being loaded onto a jet. Snuggled comfortably into a thick layer of hay, the young bird was being shipped to Sea World in San Diego inside a specially constructed crate. Scheduled to spend a few days at their splendid facility, he would soon participate in a happy ritual on a California beach. As the door of his crate opened, the welcoming ocean would stretch before him. Clumsy on land, as are all pelicans, he would soon swim gracefully and take to the air with the legendary flying skills of his kind.

BROWN PELICAN (Pelecanus occidentalis):
>   Nest: On ground, can vary from a simple scrape in soil to a platform of woven branches, 18–24 in. diam.
>   Eggs: Chalky white, scratched and soiled, 2.83 x 1.81 in.
>   Clutch size: Normally 3, occasionally 2. Single brooded, replaces lost clutches.
>   Incubation: 28–30 days, both parents.
>   Nestling: Semialtricial, naked chicks, reddish skin soon turns black. By 10–12 days, grow a coat of white down. Weight 1.58–2.80 oz. at hatch.
>   Food: Regurgitated fish.
>   Nestling period: By 6 weeks, leave nest; fly by 11–12 weeks. Parents continue to feed young for undetermined period.
>   Adult: 51 in. long, 79-in. wingspan, weight 8.2 lb. Dark-brown plumage, white head and neck. Bill and pouch marked red and yellow; colored brightly during breeding season.

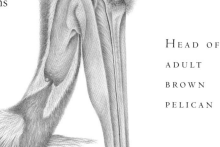

HEAD OF ADULT BROWN PELICAN

Oli

ALALA

Keauhou Bird Conservation Center, Volcano, Hawaii

Holding a mottled blue-green egg carefully in one hand, Marla Kuhn picked up a specialized flashlight and illuminated the delicate shell. Candling, done throughout the ages, was still the best way to find out if the egg was fertile. Early poultry farmers held the egg up to a candle flame to check for stirrings of life, but the modern technique is basically the same. A biologist at the Keauhou Bird Conservation Center in Hawaii, Marla was holding one of the rarest eggs on earth. Any hope that it was fertile had long since faded. Life is apparent inside an alala egg within five days; this one had been collected seven days earlier, from one of the few remaining wild alala nests left on the island. Mated pairs of birds had nearly vanished from the forest, so for two years now all of the wild eggs brought to the center had been lifeless. Turning this one slowly between her thumb

and forefinger, Marla gasped as the light silhouetted the unmistakable shape of an embryo curled within.

Many things have contributed to the dramatic decline of the alala, including habitat loss, domestic cattle, and even feral cats. Having evolved without natural enemies, these Hawaiian crows often foraged on the ground for food, where they were easy prey. Their inquisitive young also picked up fatal diseases by playing with cat scat they found on forest trails. By 1992, only twelve individuals remained in the wild; without intervention they would soon die out.

The next year, a bold plan was put in place. With the establishment of the Keauhou Bird Conservation Center, the crows gained a staff of skilled allies in their fight for survival. Biologists Alan Lieberman and Cyndi Kuehler from the San Diego Zoo were already old hands at working with critically endangered species. Alan was a former curator of birds and reptiles at the zoo, and Cyndi brought rich expertise in pioneering techniques for hatching and rearing—she had been the first to hatch a California condor in captivity. Both biologists knew that a key to the alala's future, along with habitat management, lay in removing eggs from wild nests and successfully rearing them at the Keauhou Center. Within three years, the center had enlarged the small captive alala population, creating a vital hedge against extinction. The egg-borrowing technique had little impact on the remaining wild birds, whose population in the early 1990s still included a crucial handful of mated pairs; they simply replaced their clutch with a new one.

Waiting anxiously at the foot of an ohia tree in the spring of 1996, Marla peered up at government biologist Paul Banko, who perched precariously among the upper branches. Finally level with an alala nest, he reached out to scoop up an egg and gently deposited it in a thermos filled with warm millet for protective cushioning. Then, he slowly lowered the thermos down to Marla on a rope. Loaded aboard a waiting helicopter headed for the Keauhou Center, this wild egg would soon rest in an incubator alongside those taken from captive alala nests. Seven days later, during her daily candling of all the eggs, Marla would discover the miracle held within it.

As the staff huddled anxiously over the hatching tray, the tiny emerging crow was encouraged in his struggles by recorded brood calls from adult alala. Nearly naked except for long wisps of stringy gray down, the rare hatchling lay damp and exhausted beside the pieces of his shell. Marla gently gathered up the little creature, tucked him into a soft tissue-lined nest cup, and moved him to a warm brooder. The newborn had roommates; he nestled close to other chicks from the captive flock.

Though no one guessed it at the time, the alala would never reproduce in the wild again—all of the mated pairs had disappeared. This tiny newcomer, formally dubbed Oli, which means "great joy and happiness," was often simply referred to as the miracle chick.

Thriving on a combination of cricket parts, hard-boiled egg, mouse "pups," bee larvae, and papaya, Oli now listened to recorded calls made by alala parents as they approach the nest with food. He would raise his huge wobbly head in anticipation and as he opened his beak in response to the food calls, he made a gurgling, cawing noise. If a food morsel was missed on the first try, he often flopped his head back down and simply returned to napping.

By seven days of age, Oli could see his world with newly opened bright blue eyes. The growing chick now accepted food from the moveable beak of a lifelike puppet, used to prevent him from imprinting on his human caretakers. Eagerly reaching for progressively larger pieces of mice and relished fruits, the curious youngster would soon fledge and leave his nest. Moved with the other juveniles to a large divided aviary surrounded by native trees and vegetation, Oli could also watch and hear the older alala as part of a carefully planned socialization process. In the manner of all crows, these birds are raucous and joyful communicators. Each morning, at the break of day, they welcome the sun with a special call. Thanks to the caring and skilled efforts of the Keauhou Center staff, this call hasn't been lost to the world. And, if plans go well, a wild flock of alala will once again welcome the sunrise on the island of Hawaii.

ALALA (Corvus hawaiiensis):
Nest: Each pair of birds at Keauhou Center is given a rubber tub, lined with sticks and topped with grasses, and secured to a ledge in higher reaches of the aviary.
Eggs: Pale bluish green with small dark (gray, brown, olive) speckles, 1.77 x 1.02 in.
Clutch size: Average is approximately 2.5 eggs; usually 2 clutches per year.
Incubation: 21–22 days, by female. Eggs removed from nest during second trimester and artificially incubated.
Nestling: Altricial, naked except for sparse gray down, prehistoric looking. Weight 1.02 oz. at hatch.
Food: Puppet resembling adult head used to offer a mixture of cricket parts, hard-boiled egg, mouse pups, bee larvae, papaya.

HEAD OF
ADULT ALALA

Nestling period: Chicks start "branching" (walking out of nest) at approximately 40 days, fly at 50 days. Independent at approximately 75 days.
Adults: 16–18 in. long, 24-in. wingspan, weight 1 lb. Glossy black.

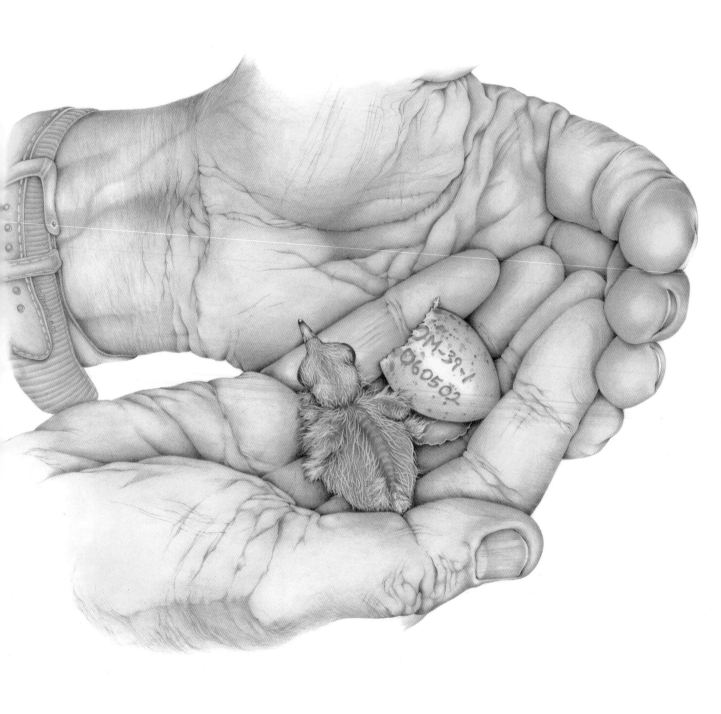

Blue 000

CALIFORNIA LEAST TERN

Project Wildlife, San Diego, California

Perched in the warm incubator, surrounded by orderly rows of speckled California least tern eggs, a tiny bright-eyed chick peered out curiously at Meryl Faulkner. It wasn't yet dawn, and she stood in stunned silence for a moment, regarding the impossibly small creature whose presence took her by such surprise. Still in her bathrobe and slippers, Meryl had slipped out to her garage for an early morning check of the eggs. This brand-new chick was a welcome, if unexpected, sight. Cotton ball-sized, its thick down had already dried. Meryl reached in gently to gather up the tiny bit of fuzz, cupping the baby protectively in both hands. Then she turned and hurried back into the house, bounding excitedly up the steps to the bedroom. Today was her husband's birthday, and as Meryl burst through the door, he sat up sleepily. At the side of the bed, she opened her hands

to reveal the squirming chick and exclaimed "Happy Birthday!"

Along its beaches, in the spring of 2002, the Naval Amphibious Base at Coronado was again playing host to a large flock of California least terns. Increasingly, these rare birds—listed as endangered since 1970—had found the quiet, uninhabited stretches of sand on the military base to be attractive nesting sites. A training ground for Navy Seals, the base faced a dilemma. As an endangered species, these small, elegant birds were federally protected; yet the military was on wartime footing, and the beaches were vital to training. Tammy Conkle, a wildlife biologist with the Navy Region Southwest Environmental Department, began formulating a plan that would be sensitive to both feathered and uniformed needs.

Tammy knew that least terns usually return to the same place where they fledged. If eggs removed from wild nests could be successfully hatched and reared in captivity, then the young birds could be released on beaches that weren't needed for amphibious military training. Tammy had worked with the Project Wildlife center in the past; they cared for injured tern chicks each spring and had extensive experience with these tiny creatures. Tammy asked the center if they would oversee the egg hatching and chick rearing.

A longtime volunteer with the center and a specialist in shorebirds, Meryl realized that the task ahead would be daunting; she was aware that nearly round-the-clock care would be required to hatch and raise these chicks successfully. Moving two incubators into her garage as part of a makeshift captive breeding facility, Meryl prepared to receive the spotted olive-colored eggs that would soon arrive.

Resting in a nest that was merely a scrape in the sand, located close to a pit used for landing exercises, the first of the California least tern eggs caught a monitor's eye early one morning. A contractor hired by the Navy, having permits to collect the eggs, she was out on a routine patrol of the beaches. Carefully, the monitor scooped up the inch-long, camouflaged orb. While cupping it delicately in one hand, she pulled an indelible marker from her pocket and jotted a date, nest, and egg number across the shell. Placing it in a portable incubator, she headed for the waiting

nursery in Meryl's garage. The next morning's patrol would turn up two of the eggs, and by the third day, eight more would appear.

Meryl meticulously weighed and candled the eggs that were neatly lined up, bathed in soft lights, and rotating slowly in perfect humidity and warmth. But predicting hatching time was impossible. Least terns incubate their eggs between nineteen and twenty-two days, but she didn't know when they had been laid. So when the first downy creature appeared unexpectedly, Meryl was surprised and delighted; but she also knew that the real work was about to begin.

As each chick hatched, she transferred it to a brooder fashioned from a plastic container. Under net-covered lids, the chicks basked warmly in the glow of incandescent bulbs. Each sported a blue braceletlike anodized band, numbered in sequence. Blue 000, the first to hatch, had taken his first food when he was only one hour old. Tern parents bring small, whole fish to their chicks to eat, and Meryl likewise offered silvery sand lances to this baby.

Growing rapidly, the youngsters soon graduated from their warm brooders to specially built backyard enclosures. Constructed of heavy netting on a pipe framework, these roomy aviaries were lined with sand and equipped with two small pools; one for bathing, the other for practicing "fishing" for sand lance morsels. When live food was introduced, goldfish and minnows, they learned to dive for it. Watching them gracefully practice flight inside their aviaries, Meryl knew they were nearly ready for freedom.

Blue 000 and four other chicks were the first of those released that summer. Of the fifty eggs collected by Navy biologists, all but seven had hatched, and nearly all had thrived under Meryl's nurturing care. Standing on Delta Beach, situated well away from the training areas on the bay side of the ocean, Meryl and Tammy joined the commanding officer of the Naval Amphibious Base at Coronado as they watched the graceful terns take flight. As she wished them luck, Meryl knew she would miss the youngsters. And two years from now, when the time came for them to return from their migrations and build nests of their own, she would be out walking these beaches, looking for flashes of their blue bands.

CALIFORNIA LEAST TERN (Sterna antillarium):

Nest: Shallow hollow in sand, constructed by female, lined with pebbles or
    pieces of shells.
Eggs: Pale olive or buff tinted, splotched with blackish brown or gray, 1.26 x .91 in.
Clutch size: Normally 2–3 eggs. Single brooded, replaces lost clutches.
Incubation: Eggs incubated by both parents, hatch in 19–22 days.
Nestling: Semiprecocial and covered with short sandy-
    buff down, mottled dark brown.
    Weight: 0.21 oz. at hatch.
Food: Small fish.
Nestling period: Both parents tend young.
    Chicks leave nest 1 day after hatching but
    remain nearby, fly at 19–21 days.
Adult: 9 in. long, 20-in. wingspan, weight 1.5 oz.
    White forehead, black cap, gray upperparts, white underparts.

HEAD OF
ADULT
CALIFORNIA
LEAST TERN

Snowy

WESTERN SNOWY PLOVER

Monterey Bay Aquarium, Monterey, California

Close to an undiscovered nest, small hands had lovingly shaped a sand castle. In their innocent beachfront play that summer afternoon, the children had not noticed the pair of snowy plovers hovering anxiously nearby in the grass. Frightened by the youngsters' boisterous squeals, the plovers finally fled, abandoning three impossibly tiny eggs that would hatch within hours.

Among the rarest shorebirds in California, snowy plovers do not build impressive nests. A simple hollow scrape in the sand lined with fragments of plants and smooth stones holds their splotched, olive-tinted eggs. But this particular nest was no secret to a dedicated band of staff and volunteers working with the Point Reyes Bird Observatory.

For twenty-five years, members of the Plover Watch have faithfully walked the beaches of Monterey and Santa Cruz Counties, care-fully monitoring nests of the fist-sized birds. Both plovers and humans inhabit these sandy stretches year-round. While people flock to the ocean to sunbathe, walk their dogs, or ride horseback, the diminutive birds are busy raising their families in a rather unusual way. Once the chicks hatch, they are abandoned by the female, who goes in search of another mate—but the father stays with his chicks for about a month, or until they have learned sufficient foraging skills and have their flight feathers. In an attempt to tip the scales for these dwindling plovers, staff and volunteers from the observatory venture forth daily like guardian angels. Late that same afternoon, a local couple on patrol spied the trio of newborn chicks, huddled together for warmth beside the crumbling walls of a sand castle.

When the downy triplets arrived at the Monterey Bay Aquarium the next morning, brightly colored and numbered identification bands already encircled each leg. Hatched with strong, adult-sized legs they would soon grow into, the youngsters looked like fluffy ping-pong balls on stilts. The color of a beach pebble, plover chicks are able to move about freely soon after hatching. Peering up curiously from their portable incubator, these orphans already had an enormous advantage; they were soon to be introduced to a special feathered resident at the aquarium called Snowy.

Four years earlier, Snowy himself had arrived as a day-old chick. Abandoned as an egg, he had also been rescued by staff working with the Point Reyes Bird Observatory. When aviculturist Bonnie Grey caught her first glimpse of the rare wisp of fuzz, she noticed that one eye was partly closed. In a quiet aviculture service room, Bonnie settled her new charge onto soft toweling in a ten-gallon tank, warmed with a lamp and heating pad. Small stuffed animals and a mirror served as roommates; seeing his reflection, the little plover felt less alone. Offerings of tubiflex worms and fly larvae, just the right size to slip down the chick's tiny crop, were eagerly accepted.

With an eye injury requiring medication several times a day, frequent handling became unavoidable. Holding the squirming baby gingerly in one hand while administering soothing drops, Bonnie was amazed at how light he was—only five grams, about the weight of a quarter. The treatments would save his eyesight, but because he was brought in as a single chick, unable to learn any skills from siblings or adults of his kind, Snowy would need to remain in captivity. Though the staff carefully avoids publicly naming resident animals and birds, Bonnie found herself unofficially calling the little plover Snowy.

The aviary at the aquarium is named the Sandy Shores Exhibit. A visual delight, it is patterned after the Elkhorn Slough, a wetland area about twenty miles north of the aquarium. Two stories high and sixty-five feet long, the exhibit includes an island, a rear and fore dune, and a small beach area with an "ocean" end complete with small waves. Transferred to this habitat as a six-week-old fledgling, Snowy soon made his presence felt.

Well known for being assertive, snowy plovers are not inclined to back down when confronted, and Snowy was no exception. A ball of energy, the chick often got himself in trouble with fearless challenges of the larger feathered inhabitants. When one of the staff remarked that Snowy was "tiny but mighty," Bonnie had to agree. Crowds of visitors noticed the little plover's antics too, and watched with fascination as he came boldly to the edge of the exhibit. Curiously, he met children's gazes eye-to-eye as they leaned in for a close look. But no one watching this feisty juvenile guessed that Snowy had a gentler destiny, as a foster father.

Four springs later, when the plover triplets arrived, Snowy was an old hand at foster care. At ten days of age, when they no longer needed the warmth and intimacy of a small enclosure, the chicks were placed with Snowy in a flight cage located behind the scenes. As Bonnie gently lowered the babies to the sandy floor, Snowy vocalized excitedly and ran to adopt them. Quickly, he became very protective of his brood, even to the point of chasing away the humans who came inside to care for all the birds.

Plover males are traditionally in charge of most parenting, and Snowy would soon be providing these fortunate babies with lessons in vocabulary, hunting techniques, and proper behavior. Armed with skills no human could impart, these three plover chicks would one day live successfully in the wild, bringing to nine the number that Snowy had prepared for freedom.

SNOWY PLOVER (Charadrius alexandrinus):

Nest: Hollow scrape in sand, lined with plant fragments. Eggs partially buried.

Eggs: Buff or olive tinted, delicate black and pale gray spotting, 1.3 x 0.91 in.

Clutch size: Normally 3 eggs, sometimes 2 or 4. Often double brooded, up to 3 broods in central California.

Incubation: Both parents, 24 days.

Nestling: Precocial, covered with creamy buff down, mottled with black. Weight 0.21 oz. at hatch.

Food: Insects, small crustaceans, bivalves, larvae, worms, gastropods.

Nestling period: Soon after hatching, young leave nest but are carefully tended by both parents. Fly at 27–31 days.

Adult: 6.25 in. long, 17-in. wingspan, weight 1.4 oz. White underparts, brownish gray wings and mantle, black bar on forecrown.

HEAD OF ADULT SNOWY PLOVER

Spud

GREAT HORNED OWL

Illinois Raptor Center, Decatur, Illinois

Once again, a conveyor belt at the Buckhart Gravel Company had been transformed into a great horned owl nursery. For the fifth year in a row, a large female had laid a pair of milk-colored eggs on the rubber belt, and incubated them round the clock. Dining at nighttime on the rabbits and small rodents provided by her mate, the owl sat faithfully on her unconventional nest for nearly a month. A large brood patch, developed especially for her incubation duties, allowed the eggs to rest next to her bare skin. Now, hidden warmly under their mother, both chicks had broken free of their shells. Only slightly larger than newly hatched chickens and weighing a mere two ounces, they were covered with pure white down. Eyes not yet open and still lacking the strength to hold up their wobbly heads, they were cradled on a dangerous ribbon of equipment that was due to be turned on within days.

Just down the road, at the Illinois Raptor Center, late March often brings with it baby owl catastrophes. Director Jane Seitz, who founded the center in 1993, wondered whether this year the mother great horned owl had chosen her nest site more wisely.

Workers at the Buckhart plant, readying the plant for spring production, approached the conveyor belt cautiously. Mother owls protect their young fiercely, and employees venturing too close had incurred this bird's wrath on an annual basis. There she was again, perched on the wide belt, glaring down with blazing yellow eyes, snapping her beak furiously. With feather ears erect and plumage ruffled out, she looked as big as a bushel basket. Retreating to their office, the Buckhart employees dialed the number of the Illinois Raptor Center.

Following a hair-raising rescue, the two tiny owlets huddled together in a softly padded cardboard box on the seat next to Jane as she drove back to the center. The snowy bundles of fuzz peeped anxiously. Jane and her staff of human volunteers would soon be calling on an expert's help to raise these chicks—a female great horned owl referred to affectionately as Spud, one of the center's permanent residents who could be relied on to be an enthusiastic surrogate mother.

Spud had never been asked to adopt chicks as young as these, but over the past several years many orphans grew to healthy owl adulthood under her watchful eye. Equally important, the lovingly cared-for young-sters took their lessons from a maternal role model who knew intimately what being a great horned owl was all about. Stepping into Spud's enclosure with the two tiny babies cupped in her hands, Jane trustingly placed them close to the large female owl. Without hesitation, Spud reached down with her pol-ished beak to tuck her new charges underneath ruffled breast feathers. One of the center's volunteers had coined a term for the female owl's tender behavior: Spud had shifted into "mommy mode."

Several years earlier, Spud herself had arrived at the raptor center in an unusual fash-ion. When Jane answered the phone one after-noon, she heard a small voice on the other end inquire about getting mice to feed his pet owl. Unaware that having a wild bird violated any laws, the child and his parents had raised Spud from chickhood. After gently explaining to the little boy that keeping wildlife was illegal without special federal licensing, Jane arranged for a rendezvous with the family. Pulling into a parking lot at the University of Illinois, she expected to see a small screech owl emerge from the family's station wagon. But with amazement, Jane watched as a huge, dignified great horned owl stepped out from her spacious carrying crate.

Though already large, Spud was still very young. Jane sometimes good-naturedly refers to owl chicks as the "Baby Hueys" of the bird world. Within weeks, they can rival the size of their parents. Eating voraciously, the youngsters relish a diverse variety of prey that includes rodents, birds, and fish. Skillfully capable of adapting to changing environments, these owls' culinary preferences can include just about anything—even skunks might be on the menu. Begging insistently with soft *hooos*, Spud was easily capable of dispatching nine or ten frozen mice daily. It was no wonder that her adoptive family called Jane in search of a steady supply of her favorite food.

Settled into an ample enclosure at the raptor center, the young owl curiously made no attempts at flight. A veterinarian's care-ful examination revealed the reason. Spud had suffered a broken wing. Likely, she fell from her nest; her young rescuer mentioned he had found her on the forest floor. Jane realized sadly that this owl would never know the legendary, silent flight of her kind. But by the next spring, it became very clear that Spud possessed special talents.

Her gentle way with foster chicks became apparent when the first of the annual owl orphans arrived, fresh from the gravel pit's conveyor belt. Because of Spud's tutelage, almost all of these babies mature and taste freedom each year. Yet, owl youngsters aren't the only ones who benefit from Spud's expansive teaching abilities. A delight to take on education programs, the enormous owl gazes back calmly at spellbound children while Jane explains the fine points of owl behavior. And with a feathered teacher called Spud, these kids may well remember their lessons about great horned owls for a lifetime.

GREAT HORNED OWL (Bubo virginianus):

Nest: Cavity either unlined or sparsely lined with available materials.

Eggs: White, smooth, with slight gloss, 2.2 x 1.85 in.

Clutch size: Commonly 2–3 eggs, occasionally 1–5. Single brooded, usually replaces lost clutches.

Incubation: 26–35 days, mostly by female.

Nestling: Altricial, covered in white down. Weight 1.21 oz. at hatch.

Food: Rodents, small mammals. Male delivers food to nest.

Nestling period: Both parents tend young; first 3 weeks, male brings food to nest. By 4.5–5 weeks, young leave nest, fly well at 9–10 weeks.

Adult: 22 in. long, 44-in. wingspan, weight 3.1 lb. Grayish to buff-brown plumage, mottled above, barred below, white throat.

HEAD OF ADULT GREAT HORNED OWL

$\mathcal{RT}$

ROYAL TERN

Animal Rehabilitation Keep (ARK), Mustang Island, Texas

RT was holding court in a parking lot, surrounded by a circle of amazed Elderhostel students. The handsome white bird stood her ground, peering boldly upward. Eyeing the women one by one, the tern opened wide her orange beak, raised the feathers in her jet-black crown, and began scolding with loud, raspy cries. Fresh off the bus on Mustang Island, the members of this birding tour were not unfamiliar with terns. But this bird's behavior seemed unusually brazen. Pulling a copy of *The Sibley Guide to Birds* out of her backpack, one of the women thumbed through its well-worn pages, wondering aloud if all royal terns were this tame.

At the Animal Rehabilitation Keep, usually called the ARK by locals on the island, Andi Wickam had just gotten a call from the Elderhostel staff about the strange standoff in their parking lot. Andi, an aviculturist at the center, had been cleaning the tern's enclosure three days earlier when RT had escaped. The sleek bird, a permanent resident of the ARK, was healthy and able to fly, but she was too tame to survive safely in the wild. Andi had watched with dismay as RT winged gracefully toward the nearby town of Port Aransas. Following a futile search, the ARK enlisted the help of the local police. There was an all-points bulletin out on Mustang Island for the feathered fugitive, complete with wanted posters placed at local businesses and restaurants. As Andi drove toward the parking lot, she hoped their runaway tern might be the cause of the commotion there.

Three years before, RT had come to the ARK as a small buff-colored chick. Royal terns are active nearly from birth; yet for much of the day, they wait patiently for their parents to return with food. A family out picnicking spotted RT huddled alone in her shallow nest on the sand, and mistakenly thought she was abandoned. Hatched only two days before, the small tern arrived at the ARK.

Looking down at the baby tucked carefully into the family's picnic basket, Tony Amos sighed. Most every spring, well-meaning beachgoers "rescued" tern chicks, but rarely were they this young. Gently scooping up the chick, Tony made his way past large water tanks that were home to a different kind of creature. Years ago, working with the University of Texas Marine Science Institute, Tony founded the ARK to treat injured sea turtles washed up on the beaches of Mustang Island. But birds and other animals also find safety at the center. As Tony stepped into a quiet back room, he smiled when he saw Diann Bunnell tending several other orphaned chicks. Royal terns were a favorite among the volunteers, but Diann had a particular fondness for the elegant birds. Reaching out to take the tiny puff, she settled the baby into a warm, towel-lined tank. As she prepared an index card with feeding and care instructions, Diann penciled Royal Tern (RT) across the top.

Because she was so young, the tiny chick required hand feeding every half hour. Diann noticed before long that RT not only eagerly accepted plump mealworms, but that she strongly associated fingers with food. The growing chick soon graduated to a diet of smelt.

But at an age when young terns usually eat independently, RT continued to insist loudly that she be fed by hand.

Soon dressed in white plumage, her wings a pearl gray, the gregarious young tern expressively raised her black crown feathers at will. Sporting a bright orange beak and black legs, she was a handsome bird indeed. Admiring her stunning charge, Diann decided it was time to move RT to the large outdoor enclosure that was home to several resident seabirds. By mingling with others of their kind, orphaned and injured birds learn avian behavior. Prior to being given their freedom, they need these essential lessons from the experts.

Diann stepped into the outdoor aviary and set RT down close to the flock, confident that the youngster would be excited to join in. But as she turned to close the door behind her, she heard loud raspy wails. Fluttering to the front of the pen, RT pleaded loudly not to be left with these strangers. After several more attempts at integration, Diann realized that because RT had arrived at the ARK at such a tender age, she identified with humans rather than terns. To meet her need for companionship, the staff began frequently giving RT the run of the center. Volunteers enjoyed her raucous company as they went about their chores, cleaning turtle tanks or preparing specialized meals from a pantry stocked with delicacies such as squid, crickets, seaweed, and mealworms. As the years slipped by, RT's playful presence became a welcome familiarity. So when she made her bid for freedom, anxious staff at the ARK worried. Not versed in the ways of wild birds, the tern would be hungry and at risk.

Relief washed over Andi as she pulled into the parking lot and recognized the escapee, still loudly demanding food from puzzled Elderhostel students. Stepping from her car and calling out the bird's name, Andi opened her arms wide as RT scurried to her with joyous cries. Clutching the runaway and sliding back into the front seat, Andi laughed as her feathered passenger hopped up on the dashboard for a good view. RT was heading home to a hearty meal.

ROYAL TERN (Thalasseus maximus):

Nest: Shallow, unlined scrape in ground.

Eggs: Creamy white to ivory, sometimes buff or greenish, heavily spotted, 2.48 x 1.77 in.

Clutch size: Typically 1 egg, rarely 2 (possibly laid by two females). Single brooded.

Incubation: Both parents; eggs hatch in 28–31 days.

Nestling: Precocial, covered with stiff down. Pale cinnamon-brown to buff, with paler underside. Weight 6.69 oz. at hatch.

Food: Small fish.

Nestling period: Leaves nest after 1 day, still tended by both parents. Chicks join flock of young that roam near adult colony. Fly at 25–30 days.

Adult: 20 in. long, 41-in. wingspan, weight 1 lb. Crown and nape feathers black, mantle and upper wings pearl gray, white underparts.

HEAD OF ADULT ROYAL TERN

Silverbell

ANNA'S HUMMINGBIRD

Wildlife Rehabilitation of Northwest Tucson, Tucson, Arizona

Cupped protectively in the man's work-roughened palm, with ample room to spare, lay an impossibly small bird's nest and its tiny inhabitant. Hummingbird chicks are completely silent, tucked into impeccably camouflaged gossamer dwellings. It was a miracle that the nest, fastened carefully in the crook of an Arizona ash tree, had even been spotted. Thanks to the sharp-eyed workman, this featherless chick had been saved from certain disaster; but her frightened mother was nowhere in sight.

Spring is a frenzied time at the Silverbell Nursery in Tucson. Trucks with tall cargoes of trees and cactus, swaying on their heavy burlap root balls, become a common sight on local freeways. Readying the ash sapling for transport, the workman had spotted a hummingbird's skillfully hidden nest as he wrestled the tree onto a flatbed truck. Now, crowded curiously around, the entire gardening crew gazed down in amazement at the abandoned chick, no larger than a bumblebee. And all were wondering how a creature this small could ever be saved.

A short drive down Silverbell Road, the Wildlife Rehabilitation of Northwest Tucson center was involved in the springtime activities of baby bird season. In the nursery room, filled with many different species of orphaned fledglings, the early morning shift of volunteers was busy responding to loud begging chirps. Deftly moving from chick to chick, practiced hands gently filled tiny gaping beaks with food. In the kitchen area Janet Miller presided over neat rows of porcelain bowls, brimming with meticulously measured ingredients including several bird formulas as well as such delicacies as minced frozen mice and plump mealworms. As carefully as a chef in a fine restaurant, Janet prepared and weighed miniature meals suited to each young diner's requirements.

Answering an anxious knock on the door, Janet gazed down at the tiny nest and its occupant cradled carefully against the man's dusty Carhart overalls. Hummingbird chicks were familiar visitors at the rescue center. Janet, along with her husband, Lewis, had established the center years ago to rehabilitate and care for injured wildlife in the Tucson area, and they had treated everything from ring cats to gila monsters. The Arizona landscape brimmed with winged residents, and there were usually a few unfortunate encounters between humans and hummingbirds during nesting season.

Before long, the quiet newcomer was tucked, nest and all, inside a green plastic strawberry container lined with soft cotton balls. By placing her in a glass-sided aquarium, the hatchling could be constantly watched, and Janet could control the warmth and humidity of her environment. The chick's own nest was a miraculous creation, hugging her tiny body like a human infant's swaddling clothes. Constructed almost exclusively of spiderwebs and only an inch high, the nest was lined with soft plant down and small feathers, and its outer wall was strengthened with lichen, bits of bark, and even miniature desert oak leaves. Flakes of turquoise paint from some brightly painted southwest windowsill completed the design.

Lingering for a moment to admire the tiny baby and her beautiful abode, Janet penciled a tag for the cage, identifying her to the staff as an Anna's hummingbird. Then, she wrote "Silverbell" in parentheses. It would be easier to identify the chick with a name during her stay at the center.

After adjusting warm lights above the little bird, Janet went to fetch some special feeding paraphernalia and mix a batch of specially formulated nectar. Hummingbirds use incredibly high levels of energy, and Silverbell would need food every twenty minutes from dawn to dusk. Taking a 1cc syringe from the shelf, Janet removed the needle and inserted a delicate piece of tubing in its place. Filling the barrel with milky colored nectar, sweet and rich in protein, she returned to the sleeping baby. Blind until they are five days old, hummingbird chicks respond to a unique signal at feeding time. Landing on the edge of the nest, the mother touches each chick behind its eye bulges with her bill. Immediately, the chicks gape, opening their mouths wide for dinner. So, Janet ever so gently touched Silverbell behind her eye bulge with a matchstick, and sighed with relief when the hungry mouth opened.

As the days passed, Silverbell grew a coat of mottled brown feathers that held a promise of iridescent green. Often called the jewels of the bird world, hummingbirds are stunningly beautiful creatures. Soon fully feathered, the growing chick began perching jauntily on the side of her elegant nest, which was surrounded by vases of cut flowers brought in by volunteers. Leaning into the cage to deliver breakfast one morning, one frequent volunteer, Fran Darnton, gasped with surprise as Silverbell rose vertically up, hovering at eye level. With wings whirring loudly, the tiny creature zipped around to Fran's ears, touching them gently with her long slender bill. Then Silverbell turned her attention instead to a jar of honeysuckle, instinctively probing for nectar. It would soon be time to free this tiny winged jewel.

Tohono Chul Nature Park, in northwestern Tucson, is a riot of wildflowers in the early spring. The morning of Silverbell's release, rehab caretakers stood alongside the tree nursery's staff, all gathered to give Silverbell a proper send-off. As Janet opened the cage door, Silverbell flew straight into the air, hovering momentarily in front of the crowd as if to say good-bye. And then, to spontaneous cheers, the tiny flash of green iridescence zipped joyfully out of sight.

ANNA'S HUMMINGBIRD (Calypte anna):
Nest: Well-constructed cup, of delicate stems, plant down, spider webs, and bits of lichen, leaves, or feathers.
Eggs: Smooth and white, matte, 0.51 x 0.35 in.
Clutch size: Normally 2 eggs; 3 broods possible during season.
Incubation: By female. Eggs hatch in 16–17 days.
Nestling: Altricial, black skin, center of back sparsely covered with gray down. Weight 0.002 oz. at hatch.
Food: Nectar and tiny arthropods, regurgitated from mother's crop.
Nestling period: Cared for by female, chicks sprout pinfeathers by 7 days, not incubated after 12 days, leave nest by 25–26 days.
Adult: 4 in. long, 5.25-in. wingspan, weight 0.15 oz. Underparts golden green, head and throat iridescent deep rose-red, underparts gray washed with green.

HEAD OF ADULT ANNA'S HUMMINGBIRD

#18

WHOOPING CRANE

International Crane Foundation, Baraboo, Wisconsin

Holding brooms for protection, two aviculturists stepped cautiously into Ginger and Bubba's enclosure. The task of gathering eggs from a pair of aggressive whooping cranes can be dangerous. Feisty by nature, they were part of a flock housed at the International Crane Foundation (ICF), a Wisconsin-based facility established in 1974 and dedicated solely to crane research and recovery. With blazing eyes fixed on the intruders, Ginger grudgingly unfolded her five-foot-tall frame and stepped away from the nest, revealing a speckled egg. Reaching down and putting it carefully into a portable incubator, the aviculturists hurried to load the precious cargo aboard a private jet bound for the USGS Patuxent Wildlife Research Center. Whooping crane chick #18 would hatch far from her birthplace at ICF.

Whooping cranes once frequented vast prairie wetlands in the United States, but by 1949, only one small flock of fifteen individuals stood between species survival and extinction. Carried on enormous wings stretching eight feet from tip to tip, these stately cranes—named for their loud, distinctive calls—were brought back from the brink by a dramatic conservation saga. And now groundbreaking efforts were under way to reintroduce a migratory flock into eastern North America. In the spring of 2002, a network of nonprofit and governmental organizations called the Whooping Crane Eastern Partnership, which included both ICF and Patuxent, was poised to stage a fall migration. The birds' unusual leader would be an ultralight aircraft.

Tucked into the wooded Maryland countryside, Patuxent's propagation center hosted a resident flock of whooping cranes. Breeding pairs had already contributed several eggs to the migration project that spring; Bubba and Ginger's offspring would represent the International Crane Foundation, and add crucial genetic diversity.

As with all whooping crane chicks, it took three long days for #18 to break free of her olive-tinted shell. With legs still folded inside her palm-sized egg, she lay exhausted and wet as she gathered strength for the final kicks that would free her. Soft purring brood calls helped stimulate the downy, cinnamon-brown chick, but whooping crane adults were nowhere near. Cradled in an incubated hatching tray, the comforting calls she heeded were recordings of parent cranes. The chick's first sight, as she opened her blue eyes, would be that of tall white figures hovering protectively above her. But they weren't whooping cranes. Under hooded costumes, Patuxent's biologists welcomed into the world a brand-new member of a species that nearly vanished forever.

Still damp and dozing, #18 now lay carefully cupped in a veterinarian's hand, her already long legs dangling through his fingers. This downy newborn would never recognize her caretakers as humans. All who came in contact with #18 would wear white costumes, with faces obscured by a Mylar screen sewn into the hood. A hand puppet resembling an adult crane's head would provide important visual cues in the imprinting process—a moveable beak, golden glass eyes, and scarlet head

patch. Whisked away to Patuxent's intensive care unit, #18 drifted off to a crane lullaby laced with the humming noise of an ultralight aircraft motor. Getting the chick accustomed to the ultralight's soothing mechanical sounds was crucial; by autumn she would be airborne and traveling behind one.

Crane chicks grow at an astonishing rate; within a month the youngster stood twenty-one inches tall, and tipped the scales at three and a half pounds. Mimicking the motions of the puppet beak, she had learned quickly to eat and drink on her own. During initial training, #18 followed an ultralight aircraft and a costumed caretaker along the ground. Because crane chicks instinctually shadow their parents, trailing the caretaker was a natural behavior. Having learned her early lessons well, the fledgling was ready now for advanced tutoring. Once more she would be a passenger on a jet plane, this time bound for the Necedah National Wildlife Refuge in central Wisconsin.

Sprawling across 40,000 acres of wetlands habitat, the Necedah Refuge provided an ideal staging ground for the planned fall migration to Florida. Their crane chick rearing facility includes large pens encompassing marshy areas. After arriving by jet from the Patuxent Center, #18 became part of a small flock of chicks that began training in earnest as they foraged for food alongside costumed aviculturists. Dragonflies, caught deftly in the mobile puppet bill, were special treats, as well as silvery smelt and red cranberries. Ultralights manned by volunteers led the youngsters on joyous romps across the grassy fields. As fall drew near, #18 and her companions honed their skills; soon they would migrate south behind their familiar mechanical companion.

A gate at one end of the enclosure led to the ultralight runway; it was here that the young cranes first took to the air. Short flights stretched to longer ones, as the graceful cranes learned to navigate skillfully behind the aircraft. They would instinctively return next spring to Necedah's familiar terrain, where they fledged. Finally, the crisp autumn air signaled that the time was right. Seventeen juvenile whooping cranes took flight that October morning in 2002 behind an ultralight, embarking on a migration that would span fifty days, seven states, and 1,228 miles. Their journey to the Chassahowitzka National Wildlife Refuge in Florida was made possible by many helping hands. Countless hours of staff and volunteer time had given these birds a chance at freedom. And the next spring, when sixteen whooping cranes returned to Necedah after soaring the eastern flyway by themselves for the first time, #18 was among them.

WHOOPING CRANE (Grus americana):

Nest: 4–5 feet across, up to 18 in. high, on the ground. Plant material added from
surrounding area. Slight depression in middle.

Eggs: Olive or creamy-buff, splotched delicately with brown or lilac, 3.94 x 2.48 in.

Clutch size: 2 eggs common, but sometimes only 1 egg laid, rarely 3. Single brooded.

Incubation: Both parents. Eggs hatch in 33–35 days.

Nestling: Precocial, covered with cinnamon-brown down.
Weight 4.38–4.55 oz. at hatch.

Food: Amphibians, fish, mollusks, crustaceans,
rodents, reptiles, insects, plants.

Nestling period: Both parents.
Chicks leave nest 1 day after hatching,
fly by 3.5 months, remain with parents 1 year.

Adult: 52 in. long, 87-in. wingspan, weight 15 lbs.
Pure white, black primary feathers on wings, dark red crown.

HEAD OF ADULT WHOOPING CRANE

ARTIST'S NOTES

I would like to pay tribute to three artists who have influenced me. My gifted twin sister, June Mullins, delights me with her mastery of color and detail, her scientific accuracy, and the humor in her art. My son Roe, whose gifted creativity encompasses his love of color and design, inspires me. And Gerald Hodge, professor emeritus at the University of Michigan, a kind and modest master of scientific illustration, creates art that never ceases to amaze me.

The illustrations of birds in this book were done in pencil, a medium I favor. Pencil allows me to add the detail I want, and is simple, clean, and honest. I try very hard to have each drawing accurately reflect the subject, in the manner of all scientific illustrators. Because of this, I work from photographs, and whenever possible I have worked from a compilation of photographs taken of the actual bird depicted in the chapter. I feel that each bird is an individual, and as such the portrait would be different in subtle ways from other chicks of the same species. The one exception is the portrait of the mute swan cygnet named Faith. Her injuries were so severe that I chose instead to portray her as she would have looked before the snapping turtle attack. The head of the adult mute swan was drawn from a photograph of Faith as an adult. To add color, I laid a transparent film over the original drawing and brushed on powdered pastels. This technique lends a hand-tinted effect rather than photographic color, and an old-fashioned quality.

Illustrations

Nest:

This illustration was drawn from a nest lent to me by Dena Moss, one of the volunteers at Bird TLC in Anchorage. It was such a beautiful little creation, and even had horsehair woven into it. The drawing is done in silverpoint, a technique that uses sharpened silver wire for the drawing tool.

Sharp-shinned Hawk (Founder):

John Parks allowed me to use some photographs he had taken in the early 1990s of sharpie chicks hatched at the Cornell Raptor Center. The hands holding the chicks are those of his wife, Robin. These chicks were some of Founder's first offspring.

Mute Swan (Faith):

This drawing was done from photographs sent to me by Pete Stevens in England.

Pete drove several hours from his home to the Abbotsbury Swannery in Dorset, and took these photos in the spring of 2003 when the cygnets were still small. Swans sometimes rest their legs atop their bodies in the water. Hope Douglas sent photographs of Faith, and the adult head drawing depicts her prosthetic bill.

Turkey Vulture (Hurlly):

Jan Goldman, a volunteer at the Pueblo Raptor Center, allowed me to draw from some wonderful photos she took of Hurlly when he was just a "fluffer." My mother had sent me a newspaper clipping of an amazing vulture chick with his wings spread out, and I couldn't get it out of my mind. The photographer at the Pueblo Chieftain who took that locally famous image, and the photo chief at the newspaper, both generously allowed me to use it as reference material for the drawing.

Sandhill Crane (Squirt):

I drew this illustration from photographs Gloria Beckman took of Squirt when he was only a few days old. The hand that Squirt is standing on is Bobby Beckman's. They were on a camping trip the weekend she took these photos, and had taken the chick along. The adult head was drawn from a photo taken by Charles Mason, a professor of photojournalism at the University of Alaska Fairbanks. The sandhills come to Creamer's Field, close to Fairbanks, to raise their chicks each year, and this adult was guarding a nest.

Bald Eagle (Hope/Liberty):

Scott Nielsen, author of *A Season with Eagles,* gave me permission to draw from his photograph of two eagle chicks. I added the art noveau touches to the nest.

Brown Pelican (Herman):

Arthur Morris, author of *The Art of Bird Photography,* is a well-known wildlife photographer who specializes in birds. The detail in his photos is exquisite, and it was a joy to draw the juvenile pelican he had captured on film. He also allowed me to draw the adult head from another of his photos in the same book.

Alala (Oli):

Cyndi Kuehler took a rare photo of a grouping of alala chicks in 1993; they were the last to hatch from wild parents. The adult head in the drawing is of the puppet the Keauhou Center uses. Cyndi, and the Zoological Society of San Diego, allowed me interpretive rights to her photograph.

California Least Tern (Blue 000):

The photo I used for this drawing was taken by Tammy Conkle, and the hands are those of Meryl Faulkner. I only realized later, when I did the research for the chapter, the significance of the numbers and letters written on the shell. I was amazed at how tiny the chick was, dwarfed by the human hands.

Western Snowy Plover (Snowy):

The Monterey Bay Aquarium generously sent me several photographs of the tiny plover chicks. Karen Jeffries, public relations spokesperson at the aquarium, graciously provided photos and information for the chapter. Plover chicks have long legs, and the photo I worked from didn't reflect that. The chick was crouched down, and the photo was taken from above, making the little creature's legs look foreshortened.

Great Horned Owl (Spud):

This photo made me chuckle just to look at it—an owl chick with a mouse tail hanging from his beak. Chris Young, webmaster and president of the board of the Illinois Raptor Center, took this delightful photo and allowed me to draw from it. Chris is also a photographer and editor for the *Springfield State Journal-Register,* which explains his talent for capturing wonderful owl images.

Royal Tern (RT):

When I had trouble locating any photos of royal tern chicks, I contacted Steve Emslie, professor of biological science at the University of North Carolina. Happily, he was getting ready to take some of his students to one of the local beaches and band chicks that weekend, and he generously offered to take some photos for me.

Anna's Hummingbird (Silverbell):

Fran Darnton, one of the faithful volunteers at Wildlife Rehabilitation of Northwest Tucson, sent me some amazing photos of hummingbird chicks. I drew from a photo of Silverbell, still in her original nest. Fran later lent me the nest to draw from—and it was such a work of art. I added the border with hummingbird eggs—they're the size of real eggs.

Whooping Crane (#18):

The photograph I used for this drawing was taken by William Weber of a famous chick named Lucky. Hatched in central Florida in 2002, he's the first wild-born whooping crane to fledge since 1939.

WILDLIFE RESCUE AND REHABILITATION CENTERS

Animal Rehabilitation Keep—(ARK)
(RT)
Mission: Dedicated to the rescue, rehabilitation, and release of injured and sick sea turtles, waterbirds, raptors, sea and land mammals.
Animal Rehabilitation Keep (ARK)
The University of Texas
Marine Science Institute
750 Channelview Drive
Port Aransas, TX 78373
(361) 749-6720
http://www.utmsi.utexas.edu/ark/index.htm

Arizona-Sonora Desert Museum
(Herman)
Mission: To inspire people to live in harmony with the natural world by fostering love, appreciation, and understanding of the Sonoran Desert.
Arizona-Sonora Desert Museum
2021 North Kinney Road
Tucson, AZ 85743
(520) 883-2702
info@desertmuseum.org

Audubon Center for Birds of Prey
(Hope/Liberty)
Mission: As an urban environmental nature center, they specialize in the rescue, medical care, rehabilitation, and release of sick, injured, and orphaned raptors. Through action-based education about the environment, they empower citizens to preserve what remains of natural Florida as well as saving the birds themselves, which has been Audubon's focus since its beginning in the 1900s.
Audubon Center for Birds of Prey
1101 Audubon Way
Maitland, FL 32751
(407) 644-0190
www.audubonofflorida.org

Bird Treatment and Learning Center (Bird TLC)
(Squirt)
Mission: Dedicated to rehabilitating sick, injured, or orphaned wild birds and offering avian education programs.
Bird Treatment and Learning Center (Bird TLC)
P.O. Box 230496
Anchorage, AK 99523
(907) 562-4852
birdtlc@alaska.net

Cornell Raptor Program
(Founder)
Mission: Established in 1993 to provide Cornell students and staff an opportunity to become directly involved in conservation of raptors (birds of prey) through educational opportunities, rehabilitation, and captive propagation and release.
Cornell Raptor Program
201 Morrison Hall
Cornell University
Ithaca, NY 14850
(607) 255-2865
www.ansci.cornell.edu/raptor

Illinois Raptor Center
(Spud)
Mission: To provide environmental education about native and migratory wildlife found in Illinois through "Education on the Wing" programs. To participate in habitat restoration through the "Partners in Education" project.
Illinois Raptor Center
5695 West Hill Road
Decatur, IL 62522
(217) 963-6909
barnowl@illinoisraptorcenter.org

International Crane Foundation
(#18)
The International Crane Foundation, where whooping crane #18 was born, works with the Patuxent Wildlife Center and the Necedah National Wildlife Refuge (among other centers) in their effort to restore whooping crane populations.
Mission: Since its founding in 1973, the International Crane Foundation (ICF) has focused attention on the conservation of the world's crane species. Based in Baraboo, Wisconsin, the foundation works with hundreds of devoted scientists and conservationists on five continents to improve understanding of cranes and the ecosystems they depend on and to develop effective conservation partnerships. Through its programs in education, research, field ecology, captive propagation and reintroduction, and professional training, the foundation has helped to ensure the survival of the cranes and their habitats throughout the world while pioneering new approaches to conservation.
Ann Burke, Director of Public Relations
International Crane Foundation
E-11376 Shady Lane Road
P.O. Box 447
Baraboo, WI 53913-0447
(608) 356-9462 ext. 147
Fax: (608) 356-9465
aburke@savingcranes.org
www.savingcranes.org

Keauhou Bird Conservation Center
(Oli)
Mission: As part of The Hawaii Endangered Bird Conservation Program, the Keauhou Center is dedicated to the recovery of endangered Hawaiian forest birds through propagation, reintroduction, and responsible habitat

management, working in concert with government agencies, public enterprise, and private landowners.
Keauhou Bird Conservation Center
P.O. Box 39
Volcano, HI 96785
(808) 985-7218
http://www.sandiegozoo.org/ cons_outpost/exp_hawaii_ud.html

Monterey Bay Aquarium
(Snowy)
Mission: To inspire conservation of the oceans.
Karen Jeffries, Public Relations
Monterey Bay Aquarium
886 Cannery Row
Monterey, CA 93940
(831) 644-7548
kjeffries@mbayaq.org

National Aviary
(Hope/Liberty)
Mission: The National Aviary works to inspire respect for nature through an appreciation of birds.
National Aviary
Allegheny Commons West
Pittsburgh, PA 15212
(412) 323-7235
www.aviary.org

Necedah National Wildlife Refuge
(#18)
W7996 20th Street West
Necedah, WI 54646
(608) 565-2551
http://midwest.fws.gov/Necedah/

Project Wildlife
(Blue 000)
Mission: Rescue, rehabilitation, release, and education. To care for injured, orphaned, and sick native wildlife of San Diego County, and release rehabilitated animals back into their natural habitats.
Project Wildlife
887½ Sherman Street
San Diego, CA 92110
(619) 449-4145
http://www.projectwildlife.org

Pueblo Raptor Center
(Hurlly)
Mission: To provide quality rehabilitation to injured and orphaned birds of prey. Also, to provide excellent educational programs for people of all ages about the birds of prey.
Pueblo Raptor Center
5200 Nature Center Road
Pueblo, CO 81003
(719) 549-2327
raptor@gncp.org

USGS Patuxent Wildlife Research Center
(#18)
12100 Beech Forest Road, Suite 4039
Laurel, MD 20708-4039
(301) 497-5500
Fax: (301) 497-5505
http://www.pwrc.usgs.gov

Wildlife Rehabilitation of NW Tucson
(Silverbell)
Mission: To provide experienced care for injured and orphaned wild birds and mammals so they can be released back into the wild.
Wildlife Rehabilitation
of Northwest Tucson
3690 Hills of Gold
Tucson, AZ 85745
(520) 643-0217

Wind Over Wings
(Faith)
Mission: To provide, through education, a personal connection with wildlife that will lead to good stewardship of the environment. In rehabilitation, the goal is to release wildlife back to their natural environment whenever viable.
Wind Over Wings
22 Old Road
Clinton, CT 06413
(860) 669-4004
Wings@snet.net

Glossary

accipiter: forest-dwelling hawks.
altricial: young that hatch in an immature, helpless condition and require care for some time.
aviculturist: a specialist involved in the care and raising of birds.

brooder: equipment that maintains a chick's environment for the first six days of life.
cygnet: a young swan.
precocial: capable of a high degree of independent activity from birth.
raptor: a bird of prey.